For a Lifetime

Principles for a Successful Marriage

JEFFREY REESE

ISBN 978-1-64140-927-8 (paperback)
ISBN 978-1-64140-928-5 (digital)

Christian Faith Publishing, Inc.
832 Park Avenue
Meadville, PA 16335
www.christianfaithpublishing.com

Printed in the United States of America

To my wonderful wife, Lisa, without whom I would be a pathetic shell of my former self.

Introduction

My wife and I have been happily married since 1980. Like all couples, we've had ups and downs, but we've never had any truly serious marital problems. This is mainly because we've built our marriage on a foundation of Biblical truth. I've listed several verses which are key to the principles that I've written about:

> Matthew 19:5 & 6 "…For this cause shall a man leave father and mother, and shall cleave to his wife: and they twain shall be one flesh. Wherefore they are no more twain, but one flesh. What therefore God hath joined together, let not man put asunder."

Ephesians 5:25 “Husbands, love your wives, even as Christ also loved the church, and gave Himself for it.”

Ephesians 5:33 “Nevertheless, let every one of you in particular so love his wife even as himself; and the wife see that she reverence her husband.”

Colossians 3:18 & 19 “Wives, submit yourselves unto your own husbands, as it is fit in the Lord. Husbands, love your wives, and be not bitter against them.”

Proverbs 5:18 “Let thy fountain be blessed: and rejoice with the wife of thy youth.”

1 Corinthians 7:3 “Let the husband render unto the wife due benevolence: and likewise also the wife unto the husband.”

Philippians 2:3 “Let nothing be done through strife or vainglory; but in lowliness of mind let each esteem other better than themselves.”

Luke 6:31 "And as ye would that men should do to you, do ye also to them likewise."

Ephesians 4:26 "Be ye angry and sin not: let not the sun go down upon your wrath."

Proverbs 12:15 "The way of a fool is right in his own eyes: but he that hearkeneth unto counsel is wise."

1 Thessalonians 5:22 "Abstain from all appearance of evil."

Whatever your religious beliefs, applying these principles will do your marriage nothing but good. This is by no means an exhaustive list of every possible thing that can keep a marriage strong. These are the principles that I have learned by practical experience and that we both try to put into practice every day. I also talked to some other couples who have had long, happy marriages and included things I learned from them. I hope that they will be as helpful to you as they have been to us.

Prologue

Courtship – Building the Foundation

All buildings, from a storage shed in the back yard to the largest office tower in the world, have a foundation of some kind. Obviously, the size and type of building will dictate the type of foundation it needs, but one thing is always true. If a building has a poor foundation, it will deteriorate and collapse much sooner than a building with a good, strong foundation. Skimping on the foundation will result in a building that requires a lot more maintenance and repair. The same principle applies to marriage. If your marriage is built on a good foundation, it will almost certainly last a lifetime. The purpose of this book is to help you build a solid foundation.

Courtship is the time preceding engagement, when your feelings for each other have ripened into love and you believe that your relationship is probably going to lead to marriage. It's when your conversations become deeper and more intimate as you try to learn as much as you can about each other. This is when you start constructing your foundation. It would be a good time to discuss the principles that I've written about. If you have these things settled in your minds during your courtship, it will save you from learning them on the fly after you're married.

In today's society, our ideas of a premarital relationship have gone a long way from what God intended. Hebrews 13:4 says, "Marriage is honorable in all, and the bed undefiled." A great many couples move in together long before they get married, and many of those don't get married at all. They're defiling the bed that God wants to keep pure. They live as though they were married, they have children, but they're not committed in the way that marriage bonds a man and a woman together. When problems arise, it's relatively easy for one or the other to bail out. Also, there are lots of couples who have lived together for years, finally get married, and then get divorced—sometimes after only a few months. Nowadays, there's no shame or stigma attached to any of this. The attitude seems to be, "What's the big deal? This is the modern age. Things are different now. This relationship didn't work out, so I'll just move on to someone else." Marriage is thought of as a cheap, disposable commodity, not the second-most precious gift after salvation that God has given us.

It's pretty much accepted today that couples will have a sexual relationship before they get married (if they even get married at all). It's considered normal and inevitable. The world abounds with people who have been intimate with a succession of boyfriends or girlfriends. Virginity is often thought of as a liability instead of a virtue. If you let it be known that you intend to remain a virgin until you get married, you will often be looked upon as hopelessly prudish and behind the times. People will say things like, "You love each other. It's perfectly natural. Go for it." "You're consenting adults. How could it be wrong when it feels so right?" "How else will you know if you're compatible with each other?"

Some of the consequences of this are well-known, such as sexual diseases, unwanted pregnancies, and single parenthood. However, there are other consequences that are not so well-known or talked about very much. One of the biggest is that having multiple sexual relationships cheapens an experience that is meant to very special. It's supposed to be what Paul

Harvey called "the ultimate embrace" between a husband and wife, not only physically, but emotionally. If you've shared this experience with others besides your husband or wife, you leave a little bit of your heart behind. You once cared very deeply for that person, but now it's over. There may regret or relief, depending on the circumstances, but it's impossible to go back in time and change things. In all of your life, there can only be one "first time." How much better for that first time to be with the person to whom you have been bonded in marriage! There's something wonderful about knowing that both of you have saved yourselves for each other. Of all wedding gifts, your virginity is the most special gift that you can give to your spouse.

If you have had previous intimate relationships, be honest and tell your wife- or husband-to-be. You don't need to share details, but it's only fair for the other person to know. It's the kind of thing that's bound to come out sooner or later. Get it out in the open now. If your spouse finds out two or three years into your marriage, he or she may start wondering what other secrets you've been keeping. It can erode your trust in each other.

Another aspect to this is that it can be very difficult not to make subconscious comparisons. This is true if you have had other partners and also if you know that your husband or wife has had other partners. One or the other of you may feel like you're getting "used merchandise." This is not to say that you can't have a happy and successful marriage, but it's like a gouge in a priceless, one-of-a-kind work of art. For the rest of your life, you'll know it's there and that there's nothing you can do to change it.

Another consequence is guilt. You may do your best to suppress it, but deep down, you know that what you're doing is wrong. It's enjoyable at the time, when you're swept away by passion. Later, though, you may think, *I wish we hadn't.* Unfortunately, once you've crossed the bridge to physical intimacy, there's no going back to where you were before. It permanently changes the nature of your relationship.

These consequences are based on what God says in His word. Any sexual activity outside of marriage is called fornication, and God has very strong things to say about it:

> 1 Corinthians 6:18 "Flee fornication. Every sin that a man doeth is without the body; but he that committeth fornication sinneth against his own body."

> 1 Corinthians 7:2 "Nevertheless, to avoid fornication, let every man have his own wife, and let every woman have her own husband."

> Ephesians 5:3 "But fornication, and all uncleanness, or covetousness, let it not be once named among you, as becometh saints."

> 1 Thessalonians 4:3 "For this is the will of God, even your sanctification, that ye should abstain from fornication."

Why does God give such strong warnings about fornication? Didn't He make us with these desires? Yes, He did, but He expects us to use them properly. As your love for each other grows, so will your physical desire. It's your responsibility to control it. God has reserved sex as the highest expression of love between a husband and wife.

As you begin your courtship, I would like to offer two important items of advice and counsel. I've learned these through my own experience as well as from the courtships of my two daughters. If you choose to follow this advice, I believe that you'll be glad you did. Also, if for some reason God shows you that it's not His will for you to marry, you'll be able to end your relationship with no regrets.

If you visit an art museum, you'll see placards everywhere saying, "Please do not touch." Often, there are also velvet ropes or something similar. Why are they there? To help you remember to keep your distance so you don't damage a precious work of art. You can think of this advice as the velvet ropes that will help to keep you from damaging the priceless intimate relationship that God wants to withhold from you until the right time. In a way, it's sort of like a wonderful Christmas gift. You know it's there waiting for you, but if you get impatient and open it too soon, the specialness will be spoiled. There's much more joy in waiting until Christmas Day to open it.

First, I suggest that you make a commitment not to touch each other before your wedding day. Don't hold hands, don't pat each other, don't touch each other at all. Paul wrote in 1 Corinthians 7:1, "...It is good for a man not to touch a woman." As your attraction grows, you'll find this more and more difficult, but don't give in. If you yield to the temptation to hold hands, it's that much easier to put an arm around each other. When you put your arms around each other, a kiss naturally follows. This will lead to more intense and passionate kissing. Each step leads to the next one, and the downward slope keeps getting steeper. With each step, it becomes more and more difficult to stop, turn around, and go back. Without ever intending to, you can very easily fall into sin. It's far better not to take that first step. Wait patiently until you're married. I promise you, the wait will be worth it.

The second item fits hand-in-glove with the first. While you're courting, I recommend that you don't ever go anywhere together without a chaperone—parent, sibling, or maybe a married friend who is God-honoring. I know the idea of a chaperone may sound unattractive and old-fashioned, but it's for your own safety. You certainly need to have private conversations, but it would be a good idea to make sure that someone to whom you are accountable is somewhere in the house, at another table in the restaurant, in the car behind yours, or somewhere else nearby. They should be within sight of you or able to walk in on you with no warning. This will make it almost impossible for you to fall into sexual sin. The key is for both of you to be committed to this throughout your courtship. Once again, I promise you that when you're married and no longer need a chaperone, the wait will be worth it.

Both of my daughters and their husbands-to-be made these commitments and stuck to them. It was hard for them, but they are very glad now that they waited. I encourage you to have the same kind of Godly courtship that they had.

Decide That the Word "Divorce" Doesn't Exist

This is something that you both should agree on long before you get married. Make a commitment that no matter what happens in your marriage, you will work together to find a solution and never consider divorce, not even casually. The key phrase here is "work together." A successful marriage takes effort from both of you. Picture this scenario: after a few years of marriage, it seems as though the two of you are going in different directions. You're unable to see eye-to-eye on more and more things. Now one of you starts to lose interest in maintaining your marriage. It feels like it's not really worth the effort. Eventually, you reach the point where you just don't care. Not about your marriage, not about your spouse. You just want to get out—often with the intention of hurting the other as much as possible in the process. Is this how you want to end up someday? Even at this stage, the marriage may still be salvageable, but it will be tremendously difficult. The one who wants to keep the marriage alive may never be able to get the other to start caring again. Don't say, "It won't happen to us." Yes, it can happen to you—if you let it.

On the surface, divorce may appear to be an easy solution to problems in a marriage. In reality, it just causes more and worse problems, especially if there are children. If you live by the rest of the principles that I write about, I can just about guarantee that divorce will never be even a glimmer on your marital horizon.

Don't Go into Marriage Expecting to Change Your Spouse

When two people meet and start to get acquainted, what they mainly see is the other's public persona. No one reveals all of him- or herself for all the world to see. People generally tend to be on their best behavior when they're out in society. As you get to know each other better, however, more of the "real you" will become visible to the other. This is, of course, how it should be. As you grow to love each other, you will want to find out more and more about the other person, and he or she will want to find out more about you. In a marriage, you will get to know each other better than anyone else on earth. You'll get to know each other's moods, feelings, attitudes, and opinions better than you thought possible. You'll never run out of things to learn about each other. You'll still have your public persona, but you won't be able to maintain an artificial "marriage persona." You may be able to do it for a while, but sooner or later, your spouse will see through it.

In a good marriage, neither one of you will want to put up a false front. You will want your spouse to know the real you. This process starts before your courtship, and it's where this principle comes into play. As you begin to learn more about who the other person really is, you may see things that should send out a warning signal. For example, the man may be a perfect gentleman when you're out in public. Behind the scenes, though, there may be a sudden, explosive eruption of temper over some insignificant thing. One of you may be a neat, tidy, organized person and notice that the other is a sloppy housekeeper who seldom vacuums the floor and lets two or three days' worth of dirty dishes pile up before washing them. One of you may be a rabid sports fan, and the other couldn't care less about sports. You may have opposing political views and feel very strongly about them. When you're in the process of falling in love, it can be easy to say about the other person, "It's a problem now, but after we're married, I'll change that." There's no question that marriage changes both partners. You have a responsibility to look after the needs of your spouse, as I'll talk about later.

You'll prefer to spend time with each other instead of "going out with the boys" or "going out with the girls." What won't change, though, is a person's basic personality. If something is a problem now, it will be a much bigger problem when you're married and living together. If a man has an explosive temper, he may do his best to keep it under control, but his wife can't make it go away. Sooner or later, he will blow up at you or one of the children. It will be like living with a land mine. You'll never know when you will trip over it and set it off. People who have this kind of temper often say things like, "Yes, I blow up, but it doesn't last long and then I calm down." Well, a tornado doesn't last long either, but look at the damage it does.

In the 1970's, there was a comedy show called *The Odd Couple*. The characters were Felix, who was a neat freak, and Oscar, who was an unrepentant slob. They were divorced men who shared an apartment, and as you might imagine, they drove each other crazy. It made for a funny show, but in a marriage, it wouldn't be so funny. If one of you is a natural slob, the other won't be able to change that. You can learn to be neater because it pleases your spouse, but it won't come naturally. There's a good chance that there will friction between the two of you, as we'll see a little later.

In the third example, the one who loves sports will probably be frustrated by the other's lack of interest, and the uninterested one will be bored by the subject. He or she (most likely she) will feel neglected during the season. There's a reason why they're called "sports widows." This isn't necessarily an insurmountable problem, especially since there are bound to be other things that you both enjoy doing, but neither one of you will be able to change how the other feels about sports.

In 1948, Norman Rockwell painted a picture called *The Great Debate*. It shows a young couple at their kitchen table arguing over Truman vs. Dewey. Their little boy is sitting on the floor under the table, crying. Imagine a scene like this at your house every election year. Most people have strong opinions about politics and will rarely change them. You certainly won't be able to force your spouse to change them.

These are just four things that could potentially cause serious problems in a marriage, but there are countless others. Of course, no two people are exactly alike. It would be a dull life and marriage if they were. What you need to do as your relationship continues is to analyze the other person's habits, quirks, and interests as dispassionately as possible and imagine living with them for the rest of your life. It would be wise to ask for input from family members and friends who know you well. They see your relationship from a different perspective and may see something in the other person that sets off alarm bells. If you find that the other person has a trait that you truly can't live with, it would be better to end your relationship now rather than go into marriage with the idea that you will change that trait.

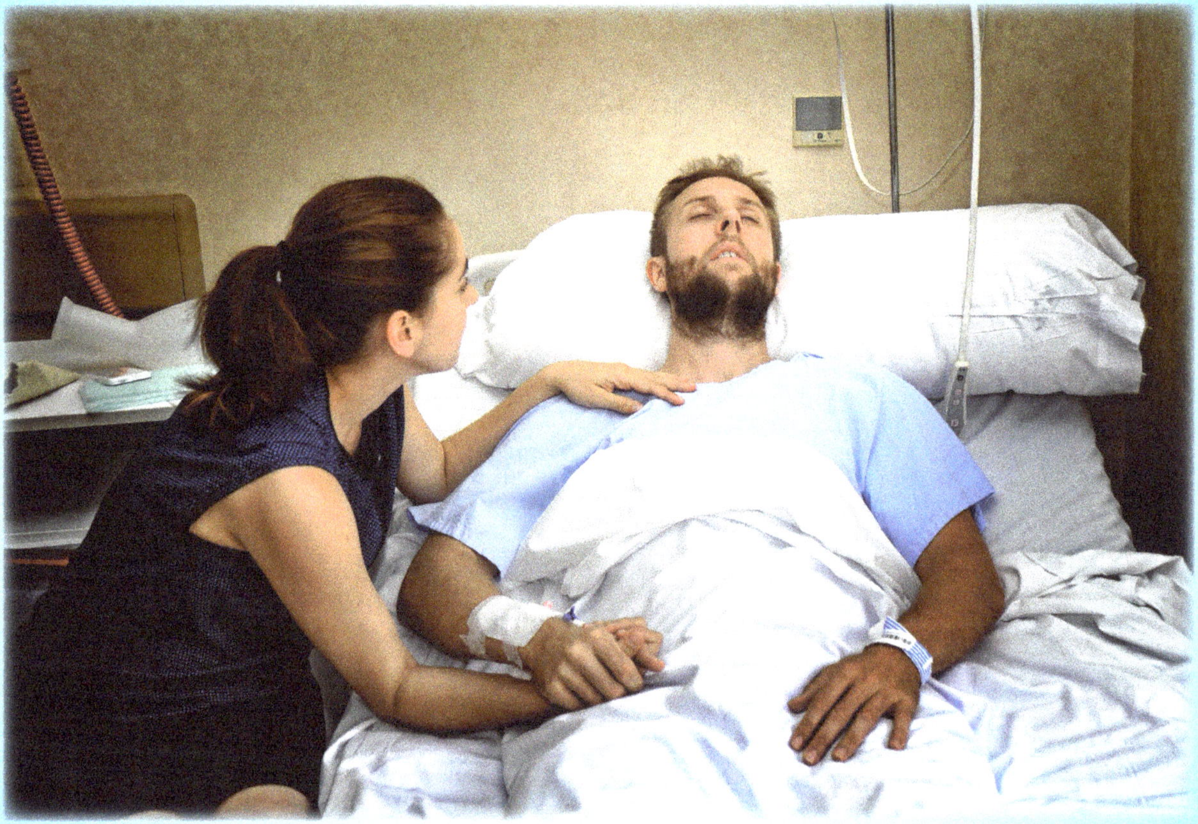

Love Is a Commitment, Not an Emotion

In the earliest stage of a marriage, you are on an emotional high. Life is full of sunshine and roses. You're walking on air everywhere you go. Your passions are high, and you can't get enough of each other. Enjoy this time and make the most of it. Remember, though, that it will not and cannot last forever. People were not designed to operate at this emotional level indefinitely. Eventually, you will come down to an "ordinary" level. Trials and problems will show up. You'll have disagreements about things. You won't always feel passionate at the same time. Many couples make the mistake of thinking that because they no longer feel like they did at the beginning of their marriage, they no longer really love each other. The husband may think that there's something wrong with him, or the wife that there's something wrong with her.

True love is not based on your emotions. Emotions change from day to day. True love is the bond that holds you together like two pieces of wood joined with carpenter's glue. When you get married, you are two halves who are joined into a solid whole. You make a solemn promise to stay together for better or for worse, for richer or for poorer, in sickness and in health, until death separates you. Before you get married, think seriously about what these vows mean. The day may come when you have a financial crisis and lose your life's savings. Your house may burn to the ground with all your possessions. One of you may become permanently disabled—paralyzed due a stroke or an accident, lose a limb, become blind or deaf. One of your children may die. One of you may get Alzheimer's disease or another form of dementia and no longer recognize the other. True love means that you stick together through trials like these. You don't give up and quit no matter how bad things get.

Yes, the "honeymoon" phase of your marriage will end. But over time, your love will grow deeper and stronger like the roots of a mature tree and will give your marriage the strength to withstand the fiercest storms.

I LOVE YOU

Say "I Love You" Every Day

This is easy when you're newlyweds, but as the years go by, you can get out of the habit. If you do, you may start taking each other for granted and gradually drift apart. Don't let that happen! Everyone wants to be loved, and they love to hear that they're loved. Telling your spouse "I love you" reinforces what he or she already knows to be true. In all of our married life, I don't think a day has gone by that my wife and I haven't said "I love you" to each other. Neither one of us gets tired of hearing it. Expressing your love every day will keep in the forefront of your mind how important you are to each other. This can also be nonverbal. Make sure you exchange hugs and kisses every day, too, if possible. They don't always have to be long and passionate. If one of you is away on a business trip, call home every evening. Tell your spouse that you're sending hugs and kisses over the phone and that you'll replace them with real ones when you get home. Even if you're passing each other while doing routine chores, reach out and caress your spouse sometimes as you go by.

Also, bear in mind that this is coupled with your actions. As important as it is to say the words, the way you treat each other says "I love you" even more sincerely. As you read these principles, you'll find that the actions I suggest are things that you do out of love for your spouse because you would never want to hurt him or her. If your actions are selfish, benefitting you more than your spouse, saying "I love you" won't really ring true. He or she may think, *You say you love me, but if you do, then why do you treat me this way?* Make sure your actions and your words back each other up.

Deal with Small Problems While They're Still Small

Don't let them grow into big problems. Problems will crop up in every marriage. The key is to take care of them right away. The ultimate cause of divorce is selfishness, but it manifests itself in countless ways. It's my belief that most divorces are not caused by one or two major crises. Most divorces seem to happen because of an accumulation of small problems that were never dealt with while they were still small. Eventually, they turn into big problems. It's an example of the adage about the straw that broke the camel's back. One straw doesn't weigh much. Two straws don't weigh much. A bale of straw weighs quite a bit. It's the same with problems in a marriage. A little problem occurs—maybe a thoughtless or hurtful word. A sincere apology and a request for forgiveness will usually solve the problem. However, if this incident isn't taken care of quickly, it can start to fester into bitterness. Later, another problem occurs and is not handled properly. Now there's a little more anger and bitterness. Multiply this by several years. Eventually, another incident happens, which is not that major by itself. Add it to ten or fifteen years' worth of unresolved problems, though, and it becomes the trigger that releases a flood of angry words and accusations like water from behind a ruptured dam. In some cases, this can create so much hurt to both the husband and the wife that it leads to the end of the marriage.

More commonly, the end doesn't happen so dramatically. The hurts slowly build up year after year, and the couple gradually grows more cold and distant toward each other. Eventually, their marriage becomes only a hollow shell. With no internal structure left, it collapses.

All of this can usually be avoided by proper communication. When one of you is angry with the other, say so in the right way at the right time. I'll talk more about this a little later. Don't keep it bottled up and say, "Well, if you don't know what's wrong, I'm not going to tell you." Big mistake. The other person may not realize that what he or she did or said was hurtful. Get it out in the open and make things right. Your marriage will get stronger, not weaker.

Attack the Problem, Not the Person

This is one of the most useful pieces of advice I've ever heard. Every couple has a few habits that annoy the other person. Sometimes these annoyances are so minor that it's not worth mentioning them. Be careful, though. This can lead to the situation I just talked about.

Other habits can become major problems very quickly. It's important to handle them in the right way. Here's a common scenario: the husband has a habit of dropping his dirty clothes wherever he happens to be instead of putting them in the laundry basket. The wife has to go around collecting them, grumbling to herself about it. As time goes on, she becomes angrier and angrier. Finally one day, she blows up. "You're such a slob. You always leave your dirty clothes everywhere and expect me to pick up after you like

I was your slave! Don't you think I have enough work to do already? You never lift a finger to make my job around here easier!"

Now the husband has been attacked, and his instinct is to defend himself. More hurtful words are exchanged and the original problem is still there. The statements, "You always…" and "You never…" are rarely true, but they can be easy to say in a fit of anger. Make a commitment not to say them.

A much better way to handle this situation before it gets out of hand would be for the wife to sit down with her husband and say, "There's a problem I'd like to talk to you about that's upsetting me very much. I would really appreciate it if you would please put your dirty clothes in the laundry basket instead of leaving them on the floor. I find myself getting angry every time I go around picking them up, and I don't want to be angry with you. I'm glad to do the washing, but it would sure make the job easier if all the dirty clothes were in the basket. Will you help me by doing that?"

This way, the problem is out in the open and no personal attack has been made. The wife has asked her husband to help her solve the problem, and most men love to solve problems. A caring and attentive husband will see that even though dropping his dirty clothes on the floor is no big deal to him, to his wife it *is* a big deal, and that it requires very little extra effort on his part to put his dirty clothes in the basket.

It can take some time to change a life-long habit. If the husband forgets and leaves his dirty clothes on the floor again, the wife can remind him, "Do you remember when we talked about putting your dirty clothes in the laundry basket? I found yours on the floor again today."

If you're a forgetful husband, find a way to keep this from happening. Post a large reminder note to yourself. Make a superhuman effort to change this habit since it matters so much to your wife.

This is just one example, but the principle applies to any problem. Personal attacks will only weaken your marriage.

Never Both Be Angry at the Same Time

Sooner or later, no matter how careful you are, one of you will get angry with the other over something. Let's take the situation with the dirty clothes that I just described. The wife has blown up and attacked her husband with hurtful accusations. The husband's first reaction is to hit back verbally. Soon, they are both furious and yelling at each other. They go out of their way to push each other's "hot buttons," bringing up past mistakes, failures, and bad choices. Later, when they have calmed down, they remember the hurtful things that they said to each other and the things that were said to them. Even after apologies, the words have been spoken and nothing can ever unspeak them. A few fights like this can do irreparable damage to a marriage.

If you are the husband in this scenario, the thing to do is suppress your desire to fight back when you see how upset your wife is. Stay quiet, listen to her, and don't let yourself get angry no matter what she says. It's like the pressure relief valve on a water heater. What she is doing is venting the pressure that has been building up inside. After a while, she will calm down and you'll be able to discuss the problem rationally. Remember, it always takes two to fight. If one of you refuses to fight, it defuses the situation at the very beginning.

This principle is equally true the other way around. If it's the husband who's angry, the wife needs to stay calm and wait until he is ready to discuss the problem.

Here's something else to keep in mind. If you are the one who is angry with your spouse, you may have any number of thoughts that you feel like saying. That doesn't mean you have to say them. It's very difficult to think rationally when you're angry, but try to ask yourself, "If I say what I'm really thinking, will it help the situation or make it worse?" No matter how angry you are, try to focus on the problem, not the person.

As I mentioned before, it's much better to take care of problems before they reach this stage, but always keep this principle in mind. It's one more tool that will help keep your marriage strong.

Don't Go to Bed Angry or Irritated with Each Other

If it's getting late and you've been dealing with a situation like the one we've just been looking at, don't go to bed while the problem is still unresolved and there is still tension between you. Neither one of you will be able to relax, and you'll feel a cold wall separating you. You may have to miss some sleep, but it's better to stay up, work the problem out, and go to bed on good terms with each other. You'll get a better night's sleep, and you won't have the problem waiting for you in the morning.

Don't Be Too Proud to Say, "I'm Sorry"

Years ago, there was a book and a movie called *Love Story*. The saying made famous by that story was, "Love means never having to say you're sorry." This is absolutely false. Love means saying you're sorry whenever it's necessary. As we've just seen, sooner or later one of you will do or say something that requires an apology. Everyone does the wrong thing sometimes. Pride is what normally keeps us from wanting to apologize when we're wrong. Humbling yourself and saying "I'm sorry" when it's needed will go a long way toward keeping your marriage strong. Sometimes, a major fight can be prevented by an early apology. Naturally, along with the apology, there needs to be a commitment to change the behavior that made the apology necessary in the first place. If nothing changes, then the apology didn't really mean anything. Apologizing and changing wrong behaviors will smooth down the rough edges and help make your marriage work with less friction.

Don't Say Disparaging Things about Your Spouse to Other People

In my experience, women are more often guilty of this than men are. I've overheard women telling other women about things their husbands did or said, and you would think that their husbands are too dumb to put one foot in front of the other without expert guidance from their wives. The thought that comes to mind is, "If this guy is such a jerk, then why did you marry him?" Everyone makes foolish mistakes and sometimes does things that turn out to be bad ideas. There's usually no reason to tell other people about bad choices that your spouse has made. Instead, tell people about your spouse's merits and virtues. The way you normally think about your spouse will influence the way you talk about him or her. If negative qualities are foremost in your mind, those are the things you'll find yourself telling to others. This habit will slowly rot your marriage from the inside out like an old, dying tree. Focus more on positive qualities, and that's what will come out in your speech. It's better to have other people wishing that they had a spouse and a marriage like yours instead of being thankful that they don't.

Never Give Your Spouse Any Reason to Doubt Your Fidelity

Many cases of infidelity happen with someone from work. You interact with these people every day and get to know many of them quite well. It's not that uncommon for an attraction to develop that goes beyond a professional relationship. You might notice that one of your co-workers seems attracted to you or you may find yourself being attracted to one of your co-workers. In either case, this should set off a loud alarm bell in your head. There's no question that it's flattering to be thought attractive by someone other than your spouse. If you find yourself in this situation, however, put the brakes on it immediately. If you don't put a stop to it right away, there is the possibility that over time, it could grow into a romantic relationship that destroys your marriage. Think of it as a weed in your garden. The best time to get rid of a weed is when it first sprouts out of the ground. If you do nothing about it, it will multiply until the weeds take over the whole garden. Don't flirt with anyone but your spouse, and don't allow anyone else to flirt with you. Also, tell your spouse about the situation. Don't keep it a secret. This is part of maintaining your trust and confidence in each other. Think about the life and bond that you and your spouse have. Is it really worth risking losing that for the sake of a fling with someone else? Those relationships rarely last for any length of time. The proverbial grass on the other side of the fence usually turns out to be thorn bushes.

When you interact with someone of the opposite sex, be careful about your surroundings. Try not to give the wrong impression to others in your workplace. Rumors spread faster than bubonic plague. Never have a conference behind a closed door when no one else is present if you can avoid it. If you need to confer privately, try to do it in an out-of-the-way spot that is still within view of other people. Don't stand too close together. To be on the safe side, keep a little more physical distance than is really necessary. Most employers have a dress code, but there's usually quite a bit of flexibility. When it comes to your clothing and behavior, don't send a signal that says, "I'm available." Don't wear clothes that are too tight or revealing. This applies to both men and women. At social occasions, like the office Christmas party, bring your spouse along. As you socialize with your co-workers, especially those of the opposite sex, introduce your spouse and try to keep him or her nearby as much as possible. Don't go off to a remote corner for a quiet conversation with someone to whom you're not married unless your spouse is by your side.

I used the workplace as an example because it applies to almost everyone, but the principle holds for any place where you regularly spend a lot of time away from your spouse—volunteer organizations, social clubs, etc. Make it obvious to everyone that you're happy with your spouse and are not interested in the charms of someone else.

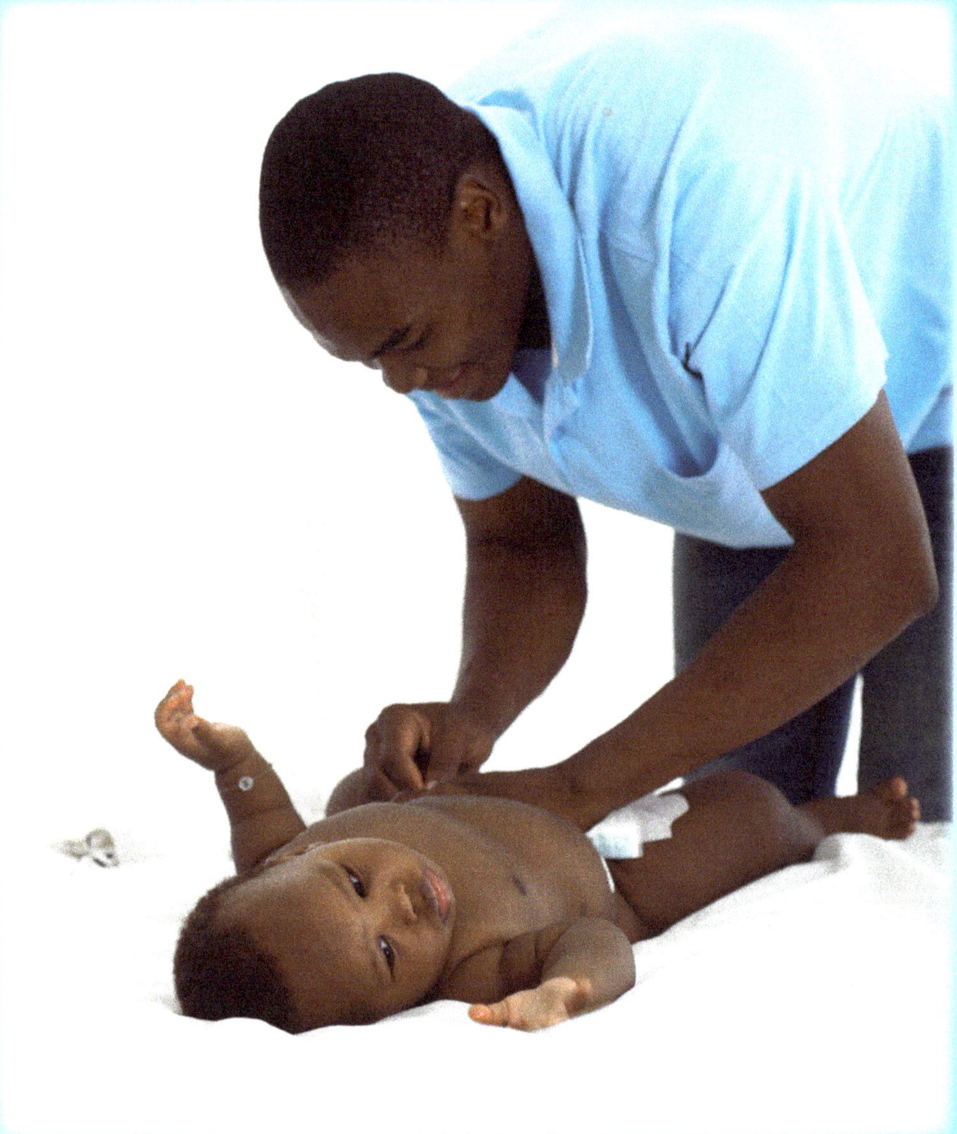

Put Your Spouse's Well-Being Ahead of Your Own

People are naturally selfish. They want things their own way and they want other people to cater to them. If this is your mind-set going into marriage, it's a recipe for disaster. One of John F. Kennedy's most famous statements was, "Ask not what your country can do for you. Ask what you can do for your country." You can apply this to marriage by changing it to, "Ask not what your spouse can do for you. Ask what you can do for your spouse." Actively look for things you can do that will make his or her life a little easier, even if it causes some personal inconvenience to you. This is especially true around the house. Wives are usually the ones doing most of the daily housework. As a husband, there are lots of things you can do that may make a big difference to your wife. Here are a few examples, but this principle can be applied in countless ways:

Try to bring as little dirt into the house as possible. Take off dirty shoes or coveralls outside and shake the dirt off there instead of bringing it inside.

Help clear the dirty dishes from the table. Work together to wash the dishes and put them away. Sometimes, say to your wife, "I'll do the dishwashing. You go and relax."

Do your share of the housecleaning. Most people are home on Saturdays. If you do the cleaning then, you both can work together and be done in half the time.

If you have a baby, take your turn at changing diapers, even the dirty ones. One of my pet sayings is, "Real fathers change diapers." You didn't mind being there while the baby was conceived. Babies and diapers go together. Changing a messy, oozing, dirty diaper is no more pleasant for your wife than it is for you. Don't be too proud to do it.

It works both ways. As a wife, look for things that you can do for your husband. For example:

If you see that your husband has an article of clothing that needs mending, do it right away, even if he says that there's no hurry.

If he has a food that's an especial favorite, make it for him sometimes even if you don't particularly like it.

Men usually get home from work at about the same time every day. If he likes to come home to a tidy house with dinner ready, then do your best to make it happen.

Let him know that you respect and support him. Men need to be appreciated by their wives. Of course, this goes both ways. Wives also need to be appreciated by their husbands.

Here is a real-world example of the application of this principle. The husband arrives at home after a long, frustrating day at work. Some days you're the windshield, and some days you're the bug. Today, he was the bug. He feels a desperate need to unburden himself and tell his wife all about the problems of the day. His wife has been home with toddlers all day and wants nothing more than to talk to an adult and tell her husband about the things she had to deal with.

A husband who puts his wife's well-being first won't just walk in and start talking about all the things that went wrong that day. He will move his problems to the back burner and encourage her to tell him about her day. Later on, he can tell her about his day.

By the same token, a wife who puts her husband's well-being first won't start unloading on him the minute he walks through the door. She will give him time to unwind, especially when she sees in his face that it hasn't been one of his better days. She will move her problems to the back burner and encourage him to tell her about his day. Later on, she can tell him about her day.

Now obviously, one of them has to be the first to start talking. If they are both putting the other's well-being first, though, this situation will turn out much better than if they both have the idea that their own needs are more important than their spouse's.

The details of every divorce are different, but if you drill through them to the very bottom, you'll find that the root cause is selfishness, as I mentioned earlier. In one way or another, the husband or the wife or both believed that what they wanted was more important. A saying that became popular in the 1970's was "Look out for Number One," referring to yourself. The idea was to take care of your own wants and needs first and then, if you have any time left over, take care of others' needs. In a Godly marriage, He has to be Number One. After that, this phrase should be modified to

"Look out for Number Two. My wife or husband is Number Two." Both of you should focus on meeting the other's needs before your own.

If both of you keep this principle in mind every day, it will be like oil in a fine piece of machinery. Your marriage will run more smoothly and have fewer problems.

Don't Expect Your Spouse to Make You Happy

This principle goes along with the previous one. Expecting to be made happy is an extremely selfish attitude, and you both will be in for a lot of trouble. If you are the one expecting to be made happy, you will be disappointed and upset when your spouse can't do it. If you know that your spouse expects you to make him or her happy, it will become an unbearable burden. Ultimately, the more you expect to be made happy, the less likely it is that you ever will be. Your spouse will always come up short.

Instead of expecting your spouse to make you happy, look for ways to make your spouse happy without expecting anything in return. Notice the difference here. This isn't a demand to receive something. It's a voluntary choice to give something. If you practice this, you will find that the more nice, unselfish things you do for your spouse, the more nice, unselfish things your spouse will do for you. Let me repeat, though, you *do not* do nice things for each other as part of a bargain: "I'll do this thing that she likes so she will do something nice for me." You do things that make each other happy because you love each other. As we've seen already, putting each other first is a major factor in maintaining a strong marriage.

Share Household Chores Whenever Possible

I touched on this a little earlier. There are very few things that are truly "woman's work" or "man's work." Housecleaning is something that has to be done regularly. Pick a day when both of you are home and do it together. Decide who is going to do which cleaning chores and learn to do them as efficiently as you can. As a wife, you'll probably have to give your husband some instructions. As a husband, listen to your wife's instructions. She likely spends more time in the house than you do and knows how she likes her environment to be maintained.

Lawn mowing is also something that has to be done regularly. Depending on the circumstances, the wife can go out and do it sometimes. If she has small children to look after, though, it may be better to leave this job for her husband. On the other hand, it could be therapeutic for the wife to go out and be alone with her thoughts while she mows the lawn, and for her husband to spend the time with the children.

Folding laundry is another thing that you can do together if you're both home. Be careful, though. If you're the husband, bear in mind that your wife may be very particular about how things are folded. Make sure you fold them the way she likes them, even if you can't see that it makes any difference. Early in our marriage, my wife and I got into a huge argument over folding towels. She wanted it done a certain way and I was doing it a different way. After things settled down, I eventually came to the realization that insisting on having my own way was foolish and that it wouldn't hurt me a bit to fold the towels the way she wanted them.

If you're a husband who is any good at cooking, take over the job from your wife sometimes. She will probably appreciate the break.

Wash the dishes together. It's often a good time to talk about things that happened during the day.

Doing these kinds of things together will strengthen the bond between you and keep your wife from feeling like the whole burden of housekeeping is on her. After all, both of you contribute to making the house messy. You both should contribute to making it neat and tidy again.

Do Your Shopping and Other Things Together

This principle builds on the last one. When it's time to go to the grocery store or run other errands, do it together whenever possible. It doesn't have to be an all-day excursion. We've found that these trips are more enjoyable when we both go. It's almost like a mini-date. You can even stop somewhere for a cup of coffee. Another benefit to this is that you can discuss your purchases as you go along. At the grocery store, it's useful to bounce ideas off of each other: "We've never had this before, but it looks good. Do you want to try it?" "We're not out of this right now, but it's on sale and we'll need it eventually. Can we afford to stock up?" You can do the same thing at the department store, thrift store, etc. Have some fun at the same time. Laugh quietly to each other about some of the ridiculous things you find for sale. Go to garage sales together, too.

Balance this with practicality, though. If all you need is a bunch of bananas, it makes more sense to stop on the way home from work and pick them up than it does to go home, pick up your wife, and then go and get the bananas.

Naturally, shopping together is more difficult if you have small children. It will be easier, though, if you plan to do your shopping when all of you can go rather than Mom taking the children to the grocery store (or wherever) by herself. If you have several stores you need to go to, you might want to occasionally plan a "shopping date" for just the two of you and arrange for a Saturday babysitter. Shopping may not be the most romantic getaway you can think of, but it can fun to do it without the distraction of your children, especially when they start to get tired and bored.

Shopping together can also forestall arguments about money. It's hard to fight about how much one or the other of you is spending when you're both deciding what to buy. I'll talk more about handling money a little later. If you're in agreement about what you're buying, it will eliminate some potential problems.

Doing things together includes more than just shopping. Go to the library, a local museum, or other places that you both enjoy. Go for a walk or a bike ride around the neighborhood. In the fall, go to a park that has lots of trees and bury each other under piles of leaves. While you were courting, you probably did these kinds of things all the time. Don't stop after you get married. Commit to making it a lifelong habit. As time goes on, you'll have more responsibilities and less free time, especially if and when you have children, but do your best to carve out time for fun things. Do them together as a family, but remember that your children will grow up and leave home eventually. When it's just the two of you again, keep on doing things together. I've heard of situations where over the years a husband and wife get so engrossed in their own separate interests that they no longer do much of anything together. He does his thing, she does her thing, and they slowly drift farther apart. Take care not to fall into this trap. No doubt both of you enjoy certain activities or hobbies that your spouse doesn't really care about, but don't let those things take over so much of your spare time that you don't have time for each other. In a good marriage, you're not only lovers, you are each other's best friend. Don't lose sight of that. Doing things together will keep your bond of friendship strong.

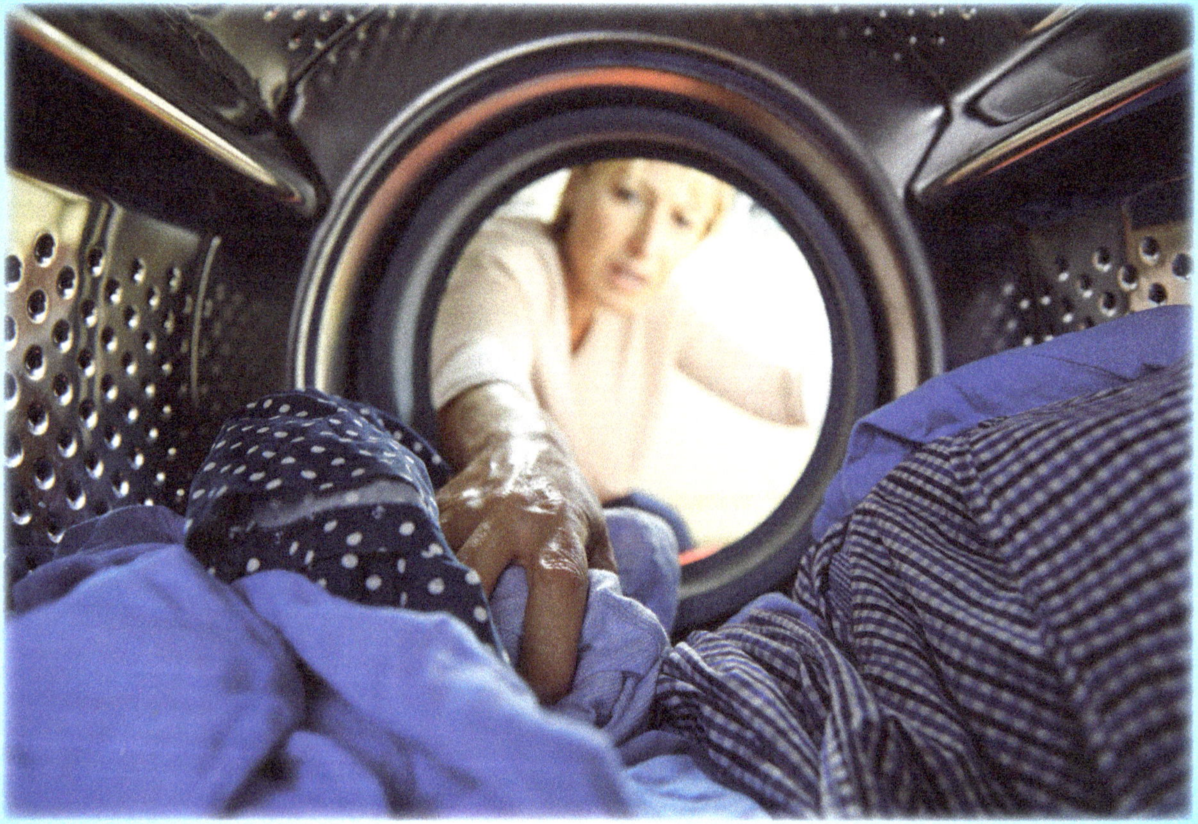

Say "Thank You" for Everyday Things

When you follow the same general routine day after day, it's easy to stop noticing the common things that the other does every day. If you're the husband, remember to thank your wife for cooking, making the bed, keeping the house clean (even when you work together), ironing, and doing other household chores. If you're the wife, thank your husband for things like working at his job, fixing things around the house, and maintaining the car. Don't let a day go by without thanking your spouse for something. Tell your spouse regularly that you appreciate him or her just for being who they are. Being thankful and appreciative will help to keep the focus on your spouse's good qualities. This in turn will influence how you talk about your spouse to other people, as I mentioned earlier.

Have Family Devotions and Pray Together

This is a great way to strengthen the spiritual side of your marriage. It's important to have your own private time of reading your Bible and praying, but it's equally important to read the Bible aloud and pray together, too. When you come to a passage you don't understand, you can talk about it and look up more information. Maybe one of you will be able to say, "I studied that myself a few months ago and here's what I learned." Sometimes you'll say, "Let's ask our pastor about this." It's one more way of increasing your knowledge and understanding of the Bible. It also increases your knowledge and understanding of each other, which will draw you closer together. You'll learn more about how your spouse thinks and feels about spiritual things.

Praying together strengthens the spiritual bond between you. It's encouraging to know that your spouse prays for you, but it adds an extra dimension to *hear* your spouse pray for you when you're together. Earlier, I discussed saying "I love you" every day. Praying for each other says it in an even deeper way. It says, "I care so much about you that I'll bring your needs to the Creator of the universe." It's kind of like going hand in hand to the throne of God. You can share other prayer needs, too. Over the years, we've gotten to know numerous missionaries, and we have a stack of their prayer cards. When we have our prayer time, we both take a card off the top of the stack and pray for those missionaries. Then those cards go on the bottom of the stack. Next time, we take the new top cards. With this system, we're able to pray for each missionary regularly without forgetting anyone.

If you have children, be sure to include them from a very early age. Even though they're too young to really understand what devotions are all about, they will grow up with Bible reading and prayer having always been a part of their lives. During your family devotion time, tailor it to suit your children's age range. Keep it short and simple for young children. Add more length and depth as they get older and can understand more. When your children are learning to read, what better thing to practice with than the Bible? Have them take a turn at reading out loud like Dad and Mom do. Encourage them to pray out loud, too. Some of the things they will pray about may sound foolish or silly, but don't ever laugh or make fun of them. You want them to develop the habit of praying about any need they may have. Ridicule will likely keep that from happening.

Since it's necessary to keep it simple with young children, the two of you might want to have an adult-level devotion time after they are in bed. After a long day, you probably won't have the energy for a lengthy Bible study, but at least spend time praying together like you did before you had children. Don't let your spiritual bond get weak. Do your best to keep it strong.

There's no one right way to have your devotions. The important thing is to make them part of your daily life. Going to church once, twice, or even three times a week isn't enough. You eat physical food more than three times a week. You need to take in spiritual food every day, too. Daily devotions are one of the most important blocks in the foundation of your marriage.

Consult Each Other When Making Decisions

Some husbands seem to feel that, "I'm the head of my house and I'll make the decisions around here. I know what's best and everyone else had better get in line!" Yes, the husband is the leader of the family and he bears the ultimate responsibility for making the final decision on family matters. It's a foolish husband, though, who won't ask for his wife's input when making those decisions. As a husband, you may think that something is a good idea. If you talk to your wife about it, she may not think it's a good idea at all, because she may see an aspect of it that you didn't see. When you look at it from her point of view, it might be that she's right and you're wrong. This doesn't make you a weak husband, it makes you a wise one. It works the other way, too. As a wife, you may have what you believe is a good idea, but your husband may veto it because he sees a problem that you didn't think of.

Here's a real-life example. Our first pastor told this story about himself several times. He was a farmer when he got saved, and he continued farming for several years before God called him to preach. It was during this period that he learned of a business deal that would require him to invest a substantial amount of money, but he was assured that he would very likely get a large return on his investment. He talked to his wife about it, and she didn't think it was a wise thing to do. She knew how hard he worked for the money they had. She couldn't put her finger on anything specific, but something about it just didn't sound right to her. He listened, but he figured that he knew what he was doing, so he invested most of their savings. Sure enough, the deal collapsed and he lost all the money. He apologized and admitted that he was wrong. To her credit, his wife didn't say, "I told you so!" He learned a valuable lesson. From then on, if she had reservations about any of his plans or ideas, he thought long and hard before he went ahead with them. Sometimes, following her advice saved them from the consequences of what would have been other bad decisions. He realized that his wife was valuable counselor to have by his side.

The important thing to remember is that your marriage is a partnership. The husband is the "senior partner," but it's not a master and servant relationship. In a business partnership, the partners consult each other all the time about how best to run the business and keep everything flowing smoothly. If one partner starts making decisions that affect the entire business without consulting the others, the business will gradually disintegrate. Your marriage is more important than any business, and it's crucial that the husband and wife work together to maintain it. You don't necessarily need to discuss every little detail about every daily situation before you take any action, but you do need to discuss your various plans and ideas. This obviously applies to major decisions such as moving, remodeling, landscaping, replacing a vehicle, or changing jobs, but it also applies to more mundane things like buying a piece of furniture at a thrift store, pruning trees and bushes, the kinds of food you buy at the grocery store, and choosing pictures to hang on your walls. Anything one of you does affects the other, so it's important to find out what each other's thoughts are. Since the two of you have been joined into a unit, decision making should involve both of you. It's one more thing that will make your marriage stronger.

Don't Have Separate Bank Accounts

The handling of money is one of the most important things to discuss before you get married. Historically, arguments about money have always ranked near the top of the list of marital problems. If one you is a tightwad and the other is a spendthrift, you will likely be in for a lot of trouble. It's better to get this out in the open long before the wedding than to find it out afterward.

As a married couple, you should no longer have "my money" and "your money." Instead, the money you earn should be "our money." You're a team, not two individuals who live in the same house. Having separate accounts will put a certain amount of distance between the two of you. From a legal aspect, having separate accounts also means that if the owner of the account suddenly dies or becomes disabled, his or her spouse will have to go through lots of legal hassles to get access to the account. With joint accounts, this problem is eliminated. This also applies to vehicle titles, the deed to your house, etc. Register them in both of your names.

In every marriage, one spouse or the other normally becomes the "Chancellor of the Exchequer," taking responsibility for paying the bills, keeping the ledger up to date, balancing the checkbook, and doing other financial chores. Whoever does this should always keep the other informed as to your financial situation. Don't be secretive with each other about your finances. There's nothing wrong with both of you having an "allowance" from your paycheck to be used at your own discretion and that you don't have to give an account for, but you should discuss purchases that are over a certain agreed-on dollar amount.

Now I'm going to go off on a different angle. Almost all married couples will have children sooner or later. Before that happens, it's fine if the wife has an outside job. After children arrive, though, it's much better if Mom is at home with them full-time. In the long run, children normally end up happier and more well-adjusted if they grew up with Mom at home rather than growing up in daycare so that Mom could have an outside career and help pay for a more lavish lifestyle. Don't let anyone get away with saying things like, "You're a stay-at-home mother? You're wasting your skills. You should be out working and making use of your talents." A full-time mother not working? Think of all the skills a mother needs. She has to be a counselor, psychologist, teacher, mediator, arbiter, purchasing manager, nutritionist, chef, and nurse. Each of these requires a college degree if you want to make a career of it. A mother has to be at least reasonably good at all of them, and she has to be able to put them to use every day at a moment's notice.

With that in mind, you should establish a lifestyle that requires only the husband's income to maintain. Instead of spending the wife's income, save it for a down payment on a house, put it into a retirement fund (it's never too soon for that), or create an emergency fund. Plan to use the husband's income for all of your living expenses. Then, when you have your first child, you won't have to agonize over how you're going to make ends meet if your wife quits her job. Living frugally can be more rewarding than having an abundance of expensive toys that need care and maintenance. Books have been written about this, so I'm not going to try to write another one here. We've been frugal all of our married lives and still live on my income even though our children have grown up and my wife has an outside job. We've never gone without anything we really needed. Overall, your marriage will likely be happier if Mom is not absorbed in her career and trying to be a good mother at the same time. Being a mother is already a full-time job, and if she has the added pressure of working at another full-time job outside the home, coupled with the need to be a good wife to her husband, she can feel like she's being spread too thin, with not enough time to do everything that needs to be done. I understand that sometimes there are situations where Mom has to take an outside job whether she wants to or not. If you find yourself in one of these situations someday, you might want to try to think of a way that she could earn money at home instead. Maybe she's a good seamstress. She could do sewing and mending for other people. A local business may need someone who can do some of their computer work at home. Maybe she loves to make and decorate fancy cakes. There's always a demand for those. Mom working outside the home should be the last resort. If she has no other option, try to find a job with hours that will allow her to be home when the children get out of school. This is a whole different subject, but if children have to fend for themselves for two or three hours before their parents get home from work, there's no end of mischief or trouble that they could get into.

Make Sure You're on the Same Page about Child Training

It's vitally important that both of you are in agreement about how to train your children. Start thinking and talking about this long before you have children, preferably before you get married. If Dad has one set of standards and Mom has a different set, the children will realize it faster than you would believe possible. They will learn quickly how to play one parent against the other. If a child asks one parent for something and that parent says, "No," the child will often go to the other parent in the hope of getting a "Yes" answer. Make sure that you agree on how best to handle this and similar situations. Even if they don't realize it, children need to know where the limits are and what they are allowed to get away with.

If the two of you have radically different sets of standards, it will cause lots of friction in your marriage. "You're too lenient!" "You're too strict!" You'll be arguing with each other, which will keep you from presenting a united front to your children and keep your children from having a proper sense of security and stability. They need to know that the rules are the same no matter which parent they're dealing with. Secure children are happier children. This is one more area where preventing cracks in the edifice that is your marriage will keep it from weakening and maybe collapsing.

Let Your Children See You Showing Affection for Each Other

This is mostly for their benefit. If your children grow up seeing you hugging and kissing, it will give them a sense of security knowing how much you love and care for each other as well as how much you love and care for them. Sometimes, you can use it as a teaching moment: "Mommy and I love each other very much, and this is how we show it. We love you very much, too." That in turn will likely carry through to their own marriages someday. They will probably not be shy about showing affection for their spouses. Of course, you have to use good judgment. Your children should never see you caressing each other in an overtly sexual way or engaging in intense, passionate kissing. That should only be done in private, behind closed doors.

In Conclusion

As you can see, having a successful marriage is not something that happens automatically. You both need to work at it every day. If you do, your chances of having a major marital crisis are much smaller. If you don't, it will almost certainly lead to divorce. Here is one more principle that applies equally to your marriage, your health, your house, and any piece of equipment or machinery: It's a lot easier to take care of it and maintain it properly than it is to neglect it until it's broken and then try to fix it. Sometimes, the damage can be so bad that it's impossible to fix. You'll have much more joy and satisfaction, and fewer headaches, if you do regular maintenance.

My hope is that you don't just read this once and file it away. Instead, keep it handy and look it over every so often. Ask yourself, "How am I doing?" Take it a step further and ask your spouse how you're doing. Give each other honest answers and work on improving things that need improvement. It's a way of doing minor maintenance in order to avoid major maintenance in the future. If you follow these principles, you will likely have a marriage that stays strong for the rest of your life and will be a shining example to your children, grandchildren, and others who know you.

Appendix

Eternity Will Be Here Before You Know It

In this book, I've quoted the Bible verses upon which these principles are based. When you follow God's directions, things will always turn out better than they will if you ignore Him and go your own way. Since we are all imperfect people, your marriage may not be perfect, but doing things God's way can make it a happy one. A happy marriage will in turn be one of the biggest factors in a happy life. Every life has problems, trials, and heartaches, but they are easier to bear if you have a caring, supportive spouse at your side. However, even the happiest life will come to an end someday, and we don't know when that will be. James 4:14 says, "Whereas ye know not what shall be on the morrow. For what is your life? It is even a vapor, that appeareth for a little time, and then vanisheth away." All of us will die and go into eternity. It's of the utmost importance that we make sure now where we will spend our eternity. After we die, it will be too late. Hebrews 9:27 says, "And as it is appointed unto men once to die, but after this the judgement." We will all stand before God someday to give an account of ourselves. There are only two possible outcomes. We will either be ushered into heaven or cast into hell. God has given us a free choice in the matter. Here is how you can make certain that heaven will be your eternal home:

> *Romans 3:10 "As it is written, There is none righteous, no, not one."*

> *Romans 3:23 "For all have sinned, and come short of the glory of God."*

If you are honest with yourself, you'll admit that you are a sinner. At some point in your life, you've used the name of God or Jesus as a swear word (that makes you a blasphemer), told a lie (that makes you a liar), or stolen something (that makes you a thief). You've probably looked with lust at a woman or a man. If you have, Jesus said that you've committed adultery in your heart. We're not sinners because we do these things. We do these things because we're sinners. We were born with a sinful nature. If you doubt that this is true, put two three-year-olds in a room with one toy and see what happens. No one had to teach you how to be selfish, deceitful, greedy, or dishonest. Since God is completely righteous and holy, He cannot allow sin into heaven. In a way, it would be like going to the most beautiful place on earth that you can imagine and dumping a load of putrefying garbage there. It would ruin it for everyone.

> *Romans 6:23 "For the wages of sin is death; but the gift of God is eternal life though Jesus Christ our Lord."*

Wages are what we earn for what we've done. Death here refers to eternal death in hell, not the physical death that comes to all of us. Since we are sinners, we all deserve to spend eternity in hell. There's nothing that we can do to earn our way to heaven. Isaiah 64:6 says, "But we are all as an unclean thing, and all our righteousnesses are as filthy rags..." The good news is in the second half of the verse. God wants us to spend eternity in heaven with Him, but it's impossible for us to get there on our own. Jesus came to earth in a human body to pay our death penalty for us. Why? Because of His love for us.

> *Romans 5:8 "But God commendeth His love toward us, in that, while we were yet sinners, Christ died for us."*

Picture this scenario: you've committed a horrible crime worthy of the death penalty. You've been convicted in court and you're standing before the judge. He has pronounced the sentence of death, but then someone else steps up and volunteers to be executed in your place. You're free to go. It's almost unimaginable that anyone would do that, but that's exactly what Jesus did. He came here to take your place and pay the death penalty of sin for you. He was beaten, flogged, and crucified. While He was on the cross, He took all of our sins upon Himself, died, and was buried. After three days, God declared the debt paid and raised Him from the dead. He went through all of that so that we wouldn't have to. We were all born sinners, so we would have to spend eternity in hell paying the price for our sins. Since Jesus is the Son of God, He had no sinful nature of His own and was therefore the only one who could take our place and pay for our sins. He did this for all of us, but there's a catch. He offers you the gift of eternal life in heaven, but you have to accept that gift. In this courtroom example, you have the freedom to accept or refuse the gift of life that you're being offered. So it is with Jesus. He offers you the gift, but He won't force it on you. If I walked up to you and offered you a hundred-dollar bill, it wouldn't become yours until you took it from me and put it in your pocket. That's what you have to do with God's offer of eternal life. You need to take it from Him to make it your own. Now, how do you do that?

> *Acts 3:19 "Repent ye therefore, and be converted, that your sins may be blotted out, when the times of refreshing shall come from the presence of the Lord."*

Repent means to turn from the direction you're going now and go the opposite way. When you realize that your sinful condition is keeping you from having a proper relationship with God, you need to be willing to turn away from it and ask Him to forgive you. Don't get the idea, though, that you have to clean up your life before you can come to God. You'll never succeed at that. Actually, it's just the opposite. God invites you to come to Him just the way you are and let Him clean up your life. He knows every nook and cranny of your heart, and He can do a much better job of cleaning it than you can.

> *Romans 10:9 & 10 "That if thou shalt confess with thy mouth the Lord Jesus, and shalt believe in thine heart that God hath raised Him from the dead, thou shalt be saved. For with the heart man believeth unto righteousness; and with the mouth confession is made unto salvation."*

> *Romans 10:13 "For whosoever shall call upon the name of the Lord shall be saved."*

Here is the final step to salvation. In your own words, in the privacy of your heart, admit to God that you are a sinner, that you know you can't save yourself, and that you accept His gift of forgiveness and eternal life. Invite Jesus to come into your heart and take control of your life. The exact words you use don't matter, and you don't have to be in church or some other special place. What matters is that you see yourself as a guilty sinner who deserves to spend eternity in the flaming fire of hell and acknowledging that trusting in Jesus is your only hope of escape. When you come to God in sincerity, He will cleanse you of your sin and make you one of His own. Your desires will change and you will want to live a life that pleases God. There are people who say, "If I became a Christian, I would have to give up too many things that I enjoy." If you fell overboard from a ship and were being dragged down by the weight of the things that you were hanging on to, you would decide very quickly that they weren't worth as much to you as you thought they were. You would gladly dump them so you could get back to the surface and be rescued. The things that God will want you to get rid of are things that He knows you are better off without. He will replace them with other things that are more fulfilling and will have eternal value. I was twenty when I accepted Jesus as my savior. There were things that I enjoyed doing, but God took away my desire for them. I don't miss them at all. Being a Christian doesn't mean that you can never have any fun. You'll find that you get enjoyment from different things. Don't let the idea of "giving things up" keep you from the joy of having eternal life.

1 John 1:9 "If we confess our sins, He is faithful and just to forgive us our sins, and to cleanse us from all unrighteousness."

God already knows everything you have ever done, but He wants you to admit it. If you come to Him with an attitude of remorse and repentance, He has promised to forgive you. What's more, He will make your heart clean and pure again, as I mentioned above. It's as if you took a bowl that was full of rotting, moldy food, emptied it, and washed it so that was clean and usable again. This isn't just a one-time thing. You may want to live a sinless life, but since you have a sinful nature, you will never be able to. Even as a Christian, you'll still mess up and do things that God says are wrong. The apostle Paul had the same problem. He wrote about it in Romans 7:15–21. If you come to God in prayer right away to make things right, you'll have a clear conscience and find that there's more joy in your life. Think of it this way: washing your dishes right after every meal is a lot easier than it would be if you let them sit for a week or more.

Hebrews 10:25 "Not forsaking the assembling of ourselves together, as the manner of some is; but exhorting one another: and so much the more, as ye see the day approaching."

As a Christian, fellowship with other Christians is extremely important. We exhort and encourage each other. Hearing sound Biblical preaching helps us all to grow in our faith, just like watering and fertilizing plants makes them grow bigger and stronger. If you are a new believer, I urge you to find a good, independent, Bible-preaching church as soon as possible, preferably one that uses the King James Bible. There are lots of other versions available, but the King James is the best and most accurate. A detailed discussion about this is beyond the scope of this book, but the Bible is called "the sword of the Spirit, which is the word of God" (Ephesians 6:17). I want the sharpest sword I can get, and I believe the King James Bible fits that description. Depending on where you live, a church that preaches sound Biblical doctrine is likely to be rather small compared to most other churches, so you may have to do some searching to find one. Here's something to watch for: Does the church have a Sunday morning and Sunday evening service, and does it also have a mid-week prayer service? This isn't an infallible test, but it's usually a good sign. Preachers who aren't afraid to call sin sin and tell their congregations what the Bible says about it generally aren't very popular, so their churches usually won't be very big. That's just the kind of preaching we need, however. We need to hear from the Bible what we ought to do and what we ought not to do. A child needs good, nutritious food to grow properly, and Christians need the good, nutritious spiritual food that the Bible provides. We need to get our toes stepped on sometimes, not just hear preaching that makes us feel good about ourselves.

Another benefit to being part of a church is having a pastor to answer your questions and be there to support and encourage you when you're having a tough time. Earlier, I listed a few of the major crises that you may someday be forced to deal with. When you feel like the weight of the whole world has fallen on you, your pastor and fellow church members can help to bear some of the weight. Even when you're dealing with life's smaller problems, your pastor and church family can be a big help. By the same token, you can be a help to someone else when they're going through trials. Maybe you've experienced the same thing that they're struggling with. Being able to say, "You know, I went through that a few years ago, and here's how I handled it" could make all the difference in someone's life.

A Final Word

In the introduction, I said that applying these principles would do your marriage nothing but good. Knowing Jesus as your Lord and Savior makes it easier to do that. Since the Bible is His word, having a personal relationship with Him means that He will enable you to apply these principles even if you feel like you can't. They will make more sense to you. As you read your Bible, I'm sure that you'll find other verses and principles that will apply to specific situations in your life and marriage. Diligently follow God's instructions, pray every day for guidance and wisdom, and I hope that your marriage will be one that other people can look to as an example of how a marriage ought to be.

Acknowledgments

A big THANK YOU to my wife, Lisa. This book wouldn't have been possible without you.

Thank you also to: Jerry and Lynn, Wayne and Sharon, Weng and Gina for your insights and suggestions. I wish that all couples had marriages like yours.

Photo Credit

Cover	vvvita
Author	Yolanda DeLoach

Page #	
8	Valerii Kalantai
18	Marcel De Grijs
22	Sean Prior
28	Marcos Calvo Mesa
32	Nikola Ilic
36	Maksim Zakharov
40	Craig Robinson
44	Dinis Tolipov

48	Wen hui Wang
50	Sean Locke
54	Jani Bryson
58	Ines Bazdar
62	Hongqi Zhang
68	Ralf Cornesse
72	Hongqi Zhang
76	Dmitriy Shironosov
80	Monkey Business
82	Gina Bringman
86	Ralf Cornesse
90	Alexander Manton
96	Monkey Business
100	Natasha Fedorova

About the Author

Jeffrey Reese and his wife Lisa have been happily married since 1980 and have raised four children. They live in central Wisconsin.

CPSIA information can be obtained
at www.ICGtesting.com
Printed in the USA
LVHW070108240419
615328LV00038B/1160/P

9 781641 409278